C0-APH-022

Thank you
to all of our
contributing authors
who made this
project a reality.

Your words are
prayerful and filled
with life. May
thousands of people
encounter God
through your act of
love.

Copyright © 2019 by Jenny Donnelly, Tetelestai Ministries.
All rights reserved. No part of this book may be reproduced, scanned,
or distributed in any printed or electronic form without permission.
First Edition: October 2019.
Printed in the United States of America
ISBN: 9781645506362

lavish

Beloved,

Journaling with the Holy Spirit changed my life.

Many years ago, I stood at the top of my stairs and realized something was missing.

Lord, I don't think I really know how much you love me.
I don't think I really get it. I am ready for the revelation.

That triggered one of the most profound seasons of my life where God would begin to saturate me with the understanding of his love for *this girl*. It was no longer enough to understand how much he loved mankind. I needed to know how much he loved *me*.

Just receive.

These words were my first instructions from him. He was asking me to set aside a moment each day to drink him in, breathe him in, and fully receive his love alone. This revelation would come through being filled daily with his Spirit, not through intellectual understanding.

No more running on empty. His Spirit overflows within me.

Journaling, doodling, drawing, writing love notes back and forth… these all became a part of my private moments with him. Sometimes, I would just lay on the closet floor with my earphones in, tears streaming down my cheeks as he washed a song over my heart. No words or drawing from me. Just tears.

I get it Lord. You love me, deeply, perfectly.

I am inviting you into the secret place where God will lavish you with words that make you blush, tell secrets that won't make sense until later, doodle images that inspire you, and hold your heart's deepest thoughts close to his.

Simply receive,

Jenny

Co-Founder & President of Tetelestai Ministries

"WRITE THE VISION; MAKE IT PLAIN ON TABLETS SO HE MAY RUN WHO READS IT."

HABAKKUK 2:2

lavish letters

How to Use This Journal

Read a letter in any order you'd like and mark it off on this page.
Lean in to the Holy Spirit. Pray, meditate, Journal, doodle, and draw.
There are no rules!

— one	— nineteen	— thirty seven
— two	— twenty	— thirty eight
— three	— twenty one	— thirty nine
— four	— twenty two	— forty
— five	— twenty three	— forty one
— six	— twenty four	— forty teo
— seven	— twenty five	— forty three
— eight	— twenty six	— forty four
— nine	— twenty seven	— forty five
— ten	— twenty eight	— forty six
— eleven	— twenty nine	— forty seven
— twelve	— thirty	— forty eight
— thirteen	— thirty one	— forty nine
— fourteen	— thirty two	— fifty
— fifteen	— thirty three	— fifty one
— sixteen	— thirty four	— fifty teo
— seventeen	— thirty five	
— eighteen	— thirty six	

Nothing Too Small

I care about every detail of your life.

Come to Me, there is nothing too small. I have come to bring you fullness of life, including the little things. I know the number of hairs on your head and I collect your every tear. I kiss your every bruise, your every bump and heal your every wound. I want you to win! I want to see you make that goal! I desire for you to be well.

I am with you through every step. I care what you are thinking about, what your heart is speaking and your every decision. Come to Me. I care about every detail of your life.

What is the value of your soul to God? Could your worth be defined by an amount of money? God doesn't abandon or forget even the small sparrow he has made. How then could he forget or abandon you? What about the seemingly minor issues of your life? Do they matter to God? Of course they do! So you never need to worry, for you are more valuable to God than anything else in this world.
Luke 12: 6-7 TPT

One

GOD ISN'T WORRIED
SO I WON'T WORRY

I Hear Praise!

In times of stress and fear, Praise Me.

In times of heartache, Praise Me.

In times of sadness, Praise Me.

You see, it's impossible to enter into praise and stay discouraged! As you praise, you will discover a love so trustworthy and radical that you stop questioning; a joy so deep that it begins to flow out everywhere you go, and a peace so overwhelming that it surpasses your understanding. I will hear your praise, and I will deliver you!

Lord! I'm bursting with joy over what you've done for me! My lips are full of perpetual praise. I'm boasting of you and all your works, so let all who are discouraged take heart…Listen to my testimony: I cried to God in my distress and he answered me. He freed me from all my fears! When I had nothing, desperate and defeated, I cried out to the Lord and he heard me, bringing his miracle-deliverance when I needed it most.
Psalms 34:1-2, 4 & 6 TPT

Two

Redeeming The Dark

I am your Redeemer!

I want to redeem every dark memory and moment of your life. I want to take the rotten places and make them smell sweet! I want to take the messy places and make them fresh and clean.

Look back at the difficult places in your journey; those places when you wondered if I was with you, or if I even saw you. Would you ask Me where I was? I want to show you.

Please invite Me to redeem your history. You will be surprised by the miracles I can work today using the worst memories of your darkest yesterdays. Allow me to be the Lifter of Your Head.

So may the words of my mouth, my meditation-thoughts, and every movement of my heart be always pure and pleasing, acceptable before your eyes, my only Redeemer, my Protector-God.
Psalm 19:14 TPT

Three

Comeback King

Where do you need My resurrection power today?

Is there a place you desire restoration? Do you need regeneration or renewal of a relationship or a dream I put in your heart? Is there a dead place in your life that needs resuscitated? Perhaps you need a complete re-launch.

I have good news: I'm King of the Comeback. There's nothing in your life that's too far gone for Me; no failure too far beyond My redemptive reach; no crushing defeat so final that I cannot apply My resurrection power, redeeming it for My glory and your joy!

The same Spirit that raised My Son from the dead lives in you, and because of this, I'm reworking your most "hopeless" situation into your greatest comeback! Speak life over these dry bones and watch as I breathe life into them once again.

Prophesy to these bones. Tell them to listen to what the Eternal Lord says to them: "Dry bones, I will breathe breath into you, and you will come alive. I will attach muscles and tendons to you, cause flesh to grow over them, and cover you with skin. I will breathe breath into you, and you will come alive. After this happens, you will know that I am the Eternal."
Ezekiel 37:4-5 The Voice

Four

DRY BONES
I WILL BREATHE
BREATH
INTO YOU & YOU
WILL COME ALIVE

Drink

I am your oasis, not a mirage.

I am real, alive, and forever closer than breath. Look up. Listen within. I am here to bring you relief in the midst of everything you are facing. I will give you more than enough to quench the dry and weary places of your heart. Nothing and no one can satisfy like I do!

Come, sit, and take shelter. I have an endless supply of strength, comfort, refreshment, healing and peace for you at this very moment. I am living water.

Drink. I am constant satisfaction for your soul. Drink. I will quench your thirst for love and belonging. Drink. I am all you need to live and flourish. Drink. You will never thirst again, because My child, I am living water s pringing uwithin you.

Your growth will draw others to My well of life, too. Thank you.

But if anyone drinks the living water I give them, they will never thirst again and will be forever satisfied! For when you drink the water I give you it becomes a gushing fountain of the Holy Spirit, springing up and flooding you with endless life!
John 4:14 TPT

Five

That Girl Is On Fire!

Have you ever noticed that you can blow out a flame, but you cannot blow out a fire?

In fact, if you try to blow out a fire, you'll cause it to grow, move faster and take more territory.

You are like that fire, My daughter. You can't be stopped or slowed down. When something or someone attempts to blow your fire out, you become stronger and more resolute in the mission I've called you to.

At times, you pick up offense, worry, fear, and disappointment. If you feel like this today, I want to encourage you! All you need is some "kindling." I am a purifier, and as you take time to sit with Me, I will burn out anything that has doused your flame until you are burning HOT again!

I have come to set the earth on fire. And how I long for every heart to be already ablaze with this fiery passion for God!
Luke 12:49 TPT

Six

Your "Yes!"

Your "YES" is unlocking the doors of your destiny!

I see your "Yes" to your friends and family. I see your strength, faith and courage to believe in the impossible on their behalf! I see you, baby girl. I see how you lay down your dreams and desires for the sake of others, and how others, both across the world and across the street, encounter My love through you.

I am going to blow you away with My radical love towards you. Trust the process, do not grow restless, and stay faithful. My timing is perfect! "Father of Eternity" is My name - I am outside of time, so do not be afraid you have missed it! I do all things well and I am so much bigger than any misstep, misunderstanding or miscommunication that concerns you. I hold your destiny securely in the palm of My hand.

I marvel at your hunger for Me and I promise, you will be filled!

Those who hunger for Him will always be filled.
Luke 1:53 TPT

Seven

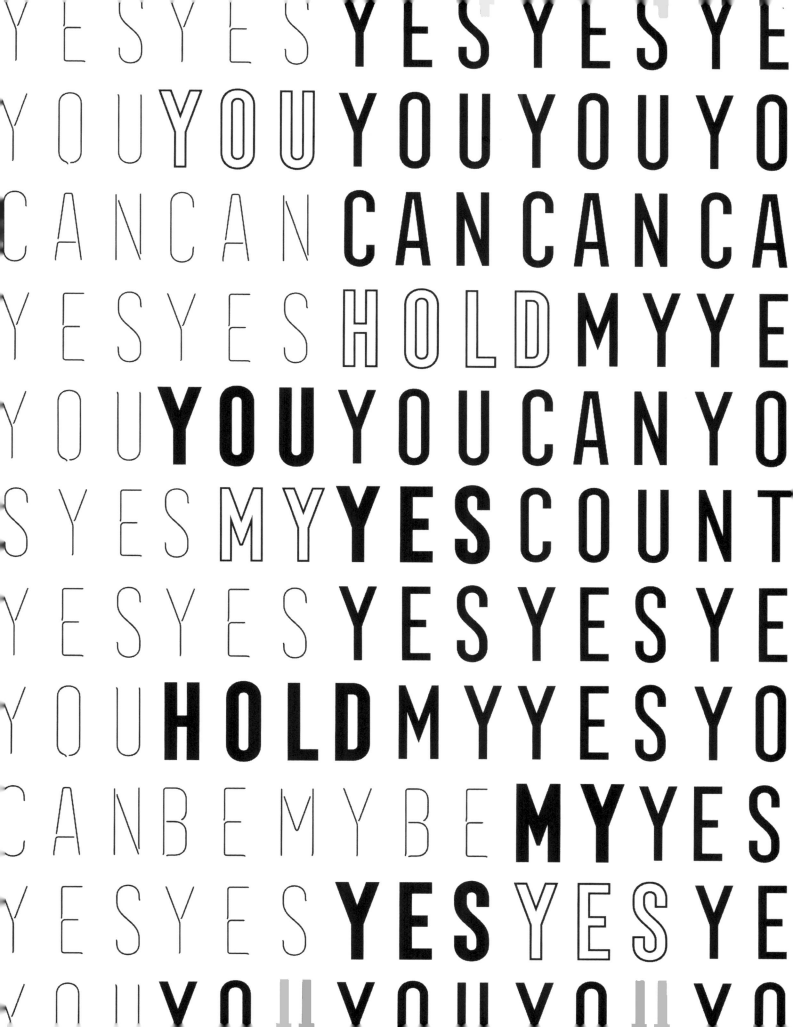

Holder Of The Keys

I hold the keys to eternal life.

The moment you learned the truth of My saving power, I unlocked your heart! It was a "suddenly" moment - your grave clothes were removed, you overcame the grave and a new glorious life emerged out of the ashes!

I continue to go, one by one, and unlock the hearts of many because I am the way, truth and life.

Did you know I have entrusted the keys to you, as well? Because you are Mine, you also hold the keys to unlocks hearts. I want to remind you of the power you possess through Me! There is a mandate on your life to pass on what you've received. I believe in you and I am so proud of you! Don't be afraid!

When I saw him, I fell down at his feet as good as dead, but he laid his right hand on me and I heard his reassuring voice saying: Don't yield to fear. I am the Beginning and I am the End, the Living One! I was dead, but now look—I am alive forever and ever. And I hold the keys that unlock death and the unseen world.
Revelation 1:17-18 TPT

Eight

Pure Pleasure

Wow! I am delighted by the purity and truth of your heart!

You so beautifully change atmospheres, powerfully releasing purity by the power of My Holy Spirit!

I want to invite you to a higher place within My presence. Come up to My holy hill and I will increase your faith to move mountains! You will learn to confidently trust the fullness of authority I have given you.

Deep in your heart today, listen for My voice speaking blessings and affirmations over you. I am delighted by you!)!

Who, then, ascends into the presence of the Lord? And who has the privilege of entering into God's Holy Place? Those who are clean—whose works and ways are pure, whose hearts are true and sealed by the truth, those who never deceive, whose words are sure. They will receive the Lord's blessing and righteousness given by the Savior-God. They will stand before God, for they seek the pleasure of God's face, the God of Jacob. Pause in his presence.
Psalm 24:3-6 TPT

Nine

Let The Tears Fall

Today is the day you realize that the tears you cry are a gift, both to you, and to Me.

At the cries of your deepest despair, I move swiftly to your heart. I pull you close to Me and pour out My soothing love over your heart like warm honey.

I am here to rescue you when your spirit is crushed, and My heart leaps with yours when you cry tears of joy! I've given you every emotion as a gift.

Don't despise this one as if it exposes your weakness - your willingness to be vulnerable actually reveals the strength I've given you!

Don't cover your face, Daughter; you're beautiful when you cry. Don't wipe your tears away. I'm catching them and meeting you exactly where you are. My love is holding onto you, and I will not let go.

You've kept track of all my wandering and my weeping. You've stored my many tears in your bottle—not one will be lost.
Psalm 56:8 TPT

Ten

Crowned By The King

If you need a King, I'm available.

If you want a crown, it's yours. If you need My oil, I'm with you. If you need My breath, inhale.

You look absolutely stunning with the crown upon your head. The jewels in your crown sparkle and accentuate your eyes. It is a perfect fit. The color of your skin and lips is perfection. Your intuition reflects My spirit.

There is no other woman like you. I fashioned and formed you with excellence, like an ironsmith. My fire softens your heart so that I can mold you. Do not squelch the fire, but instead, stand still in the midst of My all-consuming fire, knowing you are loved deeply.

Redeeming love crowns you as royalty. Your thoughts are full of life, wisdom, and virtue.
Even a king is held captive by your beauty.
Song of Songs 7:5 TPT

Eleven

Hidden in Plain Sight

I am hiding you in plain sight.

In the intimate place of hiddenness, I am opening up My heart of love to you. In the stillness of the hidden place, I am telling you the truth about who you are, and who I am.

You are like a pearl, being made uniquely beautiful in the hidden and dark place. As a pearl is shaped and perfected by irritations, you are being shaped and perfected by the shifting grains of life. As an oyster safely hides a pearl, so My wings are safely hiding you.

Under My wings, you are enough. You are protected and My healing abounds. You are receiving My strength, joy and peace. As you remain hidden under My wings, others can clearly see Me shining through you. You are beautifully hidden in plain sight.

O God, how extravagant is your cherishing love! All mankind can find a hiding place under the shadow of your wings.
Psalms 36:7 TPT

Twelve

You Are The One

Among all of my creation, you are the one I chose.

Nothing about you is random. I handcrafted you exactly the way I desired because I longed for a friend just like you. The way you laugh; the way you sing; your voice; your face… all intentionally formed and fashioned.

When you stop in your busy life and spend time with Me, it brings Me great joy. Even when you call to Me in times of despair, My ear is tuned to your voice. I recognize it among the crowds. I don't see millions at one time. I see ONE a million times over, and you are the ONE.

You are My delight, and My heart longs for sweet fellowship with you. You make Me sing! That's why I chose you.

For the Lord your God is living among you. He is a mighty savior.
He will take delight in you with gladness. With his love, he will calm all your fears.
He will rejoice over you with joyful songs.
Zephaniah 3:17 (NLT)

Thirteen

Do You See What I See?

What you said to yourself the last time you looked in a mirror may not align with how I see you.

Go back and take another look.
Do you see it? I do. You are worth the high price I paid for you on the cross! What you see when you look in the mirror is a unique display of My perfected work in making you one of a kind. I think you're beautiful. You are a living testimony I get to minister through.

Your testimony attracts people to you, and as they get to know you, they begin to see Me. You are beautiful, and Heaven is open over you. Hold your shoulders back and your head held high! I'm straightening your crown.

My old identity has been co-crucified with Messiah and no longer lives; for the nails of his cross crucified me with him. And now the essence of this new life is no longer mine, for the Anointed One lives his life through me—we live in union as one! My new life is empowered by the faith of the Son of God who loves me so much that he gave himself for me, and dispenses his life into mine!
Galatians 2:20 TPT

Fourteen

Signature Sound

Did you know I have created you with your own unique sound!?

In the same way your fingerprints reveal your identity on the earth, your voice reveals your identity to My heart. When you lift your voice in praise, it blesses Me. When you whisper My Name, it causes Me to pause and lean in. When you cry out for Me, My arms open wide and I bend low to comfort you.

Your sound is complex with highs and lows; resonance and dissonance. I hear your love, your longing, your pain and your joy together at once, and one emotion at a time. Your sound is precious and tender; kind and loving.

Your sound is full of passion and when it's coupled with Mine, it's fierce, courageous and clear! Your sound is a clarion call to the young and the old, awakening and calling forth. Your sound breathes life and births destiny. Your voice in Mine, our stories entwined, will echo My goodness across eternity. I love your voice!

"My beloved, one with me in my garden, how marvelous that my friends, the brides-to-be, now hear your voice and song. Let me now hear it again."
Song of Songs 8:13 TPT

Fifteen

Sow Lavish Love!

Oh, how blessed are YOU?!

Look around at the beautiful relationships in your life! Put down your to-do list and think about who I have given you to share your life with.
It delights me when you sow love into their lives from a place of generosity. No holding back. ALL IN.

My word about sowing generously is not limited to finances! It's about the heart of the sower. The next time you do a favor, do the laundry, make a meal, or even make love to your spouse…remember, they are a gift from My heart to yours - you get to love them first!

I will give you the grace, time, energy, and resources you need to sow into the lives of those I've given you to love, and you will have enough to passionately pursue the dreams I've planted in your heart, too! Operate in my generous JOY as you sow love, and watch the atmosphere shift!

…the one who sows from a generous spirit will reap an abundant harvest.
2 Corinthians 9:6 TPT

Sixteen

Cease Striving, Beloved

I am here to interrupt your thoughts – the ones you have about yourself.

I see you so differently than you see you. You are you are My daughter to be loved – not a problem to be solved!

Today, allow My Spirit to gently move you and shape you, rather than crushing yourself under self-judgments and plans to "fix" yourself.

Today, allow the water of My words lift and refresh you rather than driving yourself to change through discipline, self-punishment and shame.

Today, cease striving and start thriving in the fullness of life that I came to give you! Through My abundance, the self-changes you've been wanting to make will begin to take shape within you. The more you let go, the more your life, through Me, will overflow.

…I have come to give you everything in abundance, more than you expect —life in its fullness until you overflow!
John 10:10 TPT

Seventeen

Fixer Upper

I am the God of Restoration

I delight in creating new spaces, renovating areas of your life and "fixing up" neglected rooms in your heart. If you are willing to open up the door to your heart and allow me to come in, there is not an area of your life that

I cannot and will not restore!   Your marriage may be in brokenness; your finances may lie in ruin; your relationship with your children seemingly destroyed, your emotions tattered and torn… I am the master fixer-upper!

There is a process to restoration. Renovation and restoration is tedious and requires much attention to detail, but the end result is glorious! With Me as the architect of your life, you will look back and hardly recognize what your life once looked like - trust the process!

Restoration doesn't happen overnight, but once it's complete, you will not only value the end result, you will cherish the process!

God, your God, will restore everything you lost; he'll have compassion on you; he'll come back and pick up the pieces from all the places where you were scattered.
Deuteronomy 30:3

Know My Voice

Would you come be with Me?

I have so many things to tell you.
There are so many different voices from the world swirling loudly in your head.
But, no one knows you like I do.
No one can love you the way I do.

I want to tell you who you are.
I want to lead you gently.
Come, be with Me.
I want to be the most familiar voice in your head.

My sheep listen to my voice; I know them, and they follow me. I give them eternal life, and they shall never perish; no one can snatch them out of my hand.
John 10:27-28 TPT

Nineteen

I KNOW YOU & YOU KNOW ME

Perspective Shift

Sometimes, shifting your perspective is all it takes to see everything in a brighter light.

Tilt your head and heart upward and feel the warmth of My presence. By shifting your focus and thoughts from circumstances on the earth to My heavenly realm, you will gain clarity and peace.

Fix your mind on things that are true; right; pure; lovely; admirable; excellent and praiseworthy and My peace that transcends all understanding will be with you! Feast on the abundant goodness of My heavenly realm and fill your thoughts with My heavenly realities rather than the distractions of the earthly realm.

As you choose heavenly thoughts, your days will become filled with My heavenly peace, joy and hope!

So keep your thoughts continually fixed on all that is authentic and real, honorable and admirable, beautiful and respectful, pure and holy, merciful and kind. And fasten your thoughts on every glorious work of God, praising him always.
Philippians 4:8 TPT

Twenty

Grace Hurricane

II hold the keys to eternal life.

The moment you learned the truth of My saving power, I unlocked your heart! It was a "suddenly" moment - your grave clothes were removed, you overcame the grave and a new glorious life emerged out of the ashes!

I continue to go, one by one, and unlock the hearts of many because I am the way, truth and life.

Did you know I have entrusted the keys to you, as well? Because you are Mine, you also hold the keys to unlocks hearts. I want to remind you of the power you possess through Me! There is a mandate on your life to pass on what you've received. I believe in you and I am so proud of you! Don't be afraid!

The blessing of favor resting upon the righteous influences a city to lift it higher, but wicked leaders tear it apart by their words.
Proverbs 11:11 TPT

Twenty One

Fashioned For Victory

When you feel in over your head, wave My banner of victory above every high place casting a shadow over your life for all principalities and powers to see!

When you are overwhelmed, stand firm in your heavenly identity as an Overcomer. Any obstacle that stands in the way of My promises for you will be cast down by the authority of My Living Word released in your life. Sound the trumpet of victory, My powerful one!

Even My seemingly greatest defeat on the cross was simply a setup for My most glorious victory of all. If you are sharing in My sufferings, or perhaps you feel buried; hidden forevermore - rest assured. Soon enough, My resurrection power will reveal My great glory through your story. Stand firm – your most glorious victory is on its way!

Christ's resurrection is your resurrection too. This is why we are to yearn for all that is above, for that's where Christ sits enthroned at the place of all power, honor, and authority! Your crucifixion with Christ has severed the tie to this life, and now your true life is hidden away in God in Christ. And as Christ himself is seen for who he really is, who you really are will also be revealed, for you are now one with him in his glory!
Colossians 3:1, 3-4 TPT

Twenty Two

Heart Of A Champion

I am your Champion.

You are My masterpiece. A mother or a father's heart for their child is only a glimpse of the depth that I feel for you. My love for you is beyond emotion; beyond condition; beyond comprehension.

I have spent history drawing you close and revealing My heart to you. I will continue to pursue you and show you My heart. I am fiercely protective over you. You are Mine. You belong to Me… Don't be afraid to let others know how much you care - I reveal My heart through My people. Don't hesitate to accept My love through others – allow Me to make My heart known to you through them.

I have fought for you and already won. Don't fight battles that are already over. Rest in Me and listen for Me. Watch for Me in the small, unexpected ways. We are in this fully together.

Lord, you are my true strength and my glory-song, my Champion, my Savior!
Psalm 118:14 TPT

Twenty Three

Live Light

You can call on Me anytime, night or day!

If your feelings are overtaking you and the demands of life are too much to handle, release all of your stress and tension to Me. Relax into My arms and give Me every burden you've been trying to bear on your own. I will carry the weight; My shoulders are the biggest and strongest in the universe.

Meanwhile, I release you to be light, free and full of joy! I can see you now, running and skipping in the sunshine of My love.

You're not alone. So many I love are bearing heavy burdens they're not meant to carry. Would you share My compassion with them? You'll see – as you allow Me to lift your burdens, I will begin to transform other's lives through your testimony.

Are you weary, carrying a heavy burden? Then come to me.
I will refresh your life, for I am your oasis.
Matthew 11:28 TPT

Twenty Four

Celebrate The Seasons

I smile at the sight of all we're cultivating together!

Through all seasons, I am producing supernatural abundance in your life. The soil of your heart was completely replaced when you surrendered your heart to Me, and now has become the perfect place for My paradise garden to grow.

As you see how I see, you will not despise winter's "unseen" growth, but instead, rejoice in the forming of new, healthy roots! You will no longer see spring's tiny buds as "too small," but rather, as hopeful signs of a fresh start.

Tenderly and powerfully, I'm touching every seed within you to flourish in its proper time. Let's celebrate the seasons of your growth together! Your inward life is sprouting, bringing forth fruit.

What a beautiful paradise unfolds within you. When I'm near you, I smell aromas of the finest spice for many clusters of my exquisite fruit now grow within your inner garden.
Song of Songs 4:13-14 TPT

Twenty Five

A beautiful Paradise unfolds Within Me.

How May I Help You?

How may I help you?

Drop your worries off at My doorstep and I will deal with them accordingly. It is My pleasure to work things out for you!

Imagine you're traveling through the airport with a good friend and you have an uncomfortably heavy bag to carry. A good friend would offer to carry it for you! Because you know they love you, you would receive their help. Even if you should lose sight of them along the way, you could trust that your luggage will end up at the right destination because your friend cares for the things that concern you.

Oh dear child, can you trust Me like this with your burdens? Will you release your worries to Me and trust that I know your final destination? I have a beautiful plan for you. I want to take your weighty baggage and carry it for you – it's actually My pleasure!

You can trust Me with the things that concern you. The same joy and r elief you feel when a friend carries your luggage through the airport can be found in allowing Me to carry the burdens of your heart.

O God, how extravagant is your cherishing love! All mankind can find a hiding place under the shadow of your wings.
Psalms 36:7 TPT

I Chose You!

Before the foundations of the world, I looked into eternity and fastened My gaze upon you.

It's My joy to give you My wisdom, counsel and instruction, so please don't My heart of love opened toward you and I deliberately chose you, that I might know you and lavish you with love.

When I gaze upon, I want you to receive all that I have for you. I have placed on your head a crown of honor and glory. My goodness is limitless and My love for you is relentless!
I
 love you with perfect singularity. I love you just for you, just the way you are, unrefined and unfinished. I love you forever: before time began, before you took your first breath, and after you take your last. I love you perfectly and forever. You are a delight to My heart.

No one else will ever love you with every cell, fiber and breath like I do. I love you furiously, intensely and unconditionally.
Hear these words and believe them. Trust My words and let them raise you to the mountaintop. You did not choose Me, but I chose you!

You did not choose Me, but I chose you!
You didn't choose Me, but I've chosen and commissioned
you to go into the world and bear fruit.
John 15:16 TPT

Twenty Seven

Arise

Arise in the aroma of My grace, Beautiful.

I have come to make beauty from your ashes. Watch Me create beauty from what you thought was the worst mistake of your life! No more beating yourself up, thinking you are not worthy of beauty. You are worthy.

So, My Daughter, surrender your heavy layers of guilt, shame, depression, loneliness, and unbelief and put on the garment of praise! Let My oil of joy pour over you and dance with Me in full Surrender! My way is full of ease; it's so light! As you arise out of the ashes, you will feel hope rising up inside you.

Here is My hand - grab it. Let's go on our next adventure together! Arise in splendor and be radiant; My Glory will stream from you, leading others to Me!

I am sent to announce a new season of Yahweh's grace and a time of God's recompense on his enemies, to comfort all who are in sorrow, to strengthen those crushed by despair who mourn in Zion-to give them a beautiful bouquet in the place of ashes, the oil of bliss instead of tears, and the mantle of joyous praise instead of the spirit of heaviness. Because of this, they will be known as Mighty Oaks of Righteousness planted by Yahweh as a living display of his glory.
Isaiah 61:2-3

Twenty Eight

I See Myself In You!

I am in awe of you, My Radiant One!

My transformational love spills out of you in such abundant ways! Don't underestimate your smile. Don't underestimate your kindness. Don't underestimate the way your presence shifts the atmosphere. Don't underestimate the impact of your humility, honor and grace. As I am, you are! If it's true of Me, it's true of you.

I release and declare the inheritance of My nature within you. By the power of My Spirit, you will believe the truth about you in a new ways. Today, walk with your shoulders back and your head held high, knowing that as you remain in Me, so I remain in you.

I am the sprouting vine and you're my branches. As you live in union with me as your source, fruitfulness will stream from within you.
John 15:5 TPT

Twenty Nine

Purposely, Perfectly Made

I want to help you grasp the importance of your perfectly unique design.

Picture this: the angles rejoiced with Me as you entered the world! It's true! Your smile, your laugh, and the melody of your voice were orchestrated for My joy and your purpose!

You wouldn't be any better, or do any better, if you were taller or shorter. You wouldn't gain more of My love or favor if you had darker or lighter skin or hair.

You've heard Me say this before, but this time, let it take root: you were intentionally created by My hand to fulfill exactly what I've destined you to do!

We have become his poetry, a created people that will fulfill the destiny he has given each of us, for we are joined to Jesus, the Anointed One. Even before we were born, God planned in advance out destiny and the good works we would do to fulfill it!
Ephesians 2:10 TPT

Thirty

Tear the Roof off!

Your breakthrough is here and your time is now!

It's time to bust through the invisible roof – the one that has set itself up over your next-level blessings! This roof is made up of small thoughts disguised as the truth. They're not thoughts I would think, so even if they're fact, they're still not The Truth!

Let Me help you identify this faulty roof system and together, we will completely demolish these lies and reconstruct your belief system using My Word. I'm going to teach you to think the way I think, and as you learn, My next-level promises and plans will unfold in your life.

Let's tear this roof off!

We can demolish every deceptive fantasy that opposes God and break through every arrogant attitude that is raised up in defiance of the true knowledge of God. We capture, like prisoners of war, every thought, and insist that it bow in obedience to the Anointed One.
2 Corinthians 10:5 TPT

Thirty One

WE CAN DEMOLISH EVERY DECEPTIVE FANTASY THAT OPPOSES GOD AND BREAK THROUGH EVERY ARROGANT ATTITUDE THAT IS RAISED UP IN DEFIANCE OF THE TRUE KNOWLEDGE OF GOD.

Legacy of Love

My gaze is fixed upon you.

When your eyes glance away under the weight of My nearness, I want to remind you—you can't mess this up. You're not a passing phase, you're My prize and passion!

When I look upon you, I don't make account of the places you've not yet been, your age, or even the unbelief that, at times, tries to steal your attention. No— I see your Spirit that has journeyed into unknown adventures with Me, free falling in My love! I soak in the praises of your lips. Your lifetime of love has exhilarated Me!

Our unity in every season has prepared you to pass on the heritage of our love to those coming after you. You, My forever love, are Mothering the Nations!

When I look at you, I see your inner strength, so stately and strong…your virtues and grace cause a thousand famous soldiers to surrender to your beauty. Your pure faith and love rest over your heart as you nurture those who are yet infants.
Song of Songs 4:4-5 TPT

Thirty Two

Champion. Father. Friend

Where do you need My resurrection power today?

Is there a place you desire restoration? Do you need regeneration or renewal of a relationship or a dream I put in your heart? Is there a dead place in your life that needs resuscitated? Perhaps you need a complete re-launch.
I have good news: I'm King of the Comeback. There's nothing in your life that's too far gone for Me; no failure too far beyond My redemptive reach; no crushing defeat so final that I cannot apply My resurrection power, redeeming it for My glory and your joy!

The same Spirit that raised My Son from the dead lives in you, and because of this, I'm reworking your most "hopeless" situation into your greatest comeback! Speak life over these dry bones and watch as I breathe life into them once again.

Prophesy to these bones. Tell them to listen to what the Eternal Lord says to them: "Dry bones, I will breathe breath into you, and you will come alive. I will attach muscles and tendons to you, cause flesh to grow over them, and cover you with skin. I will breathe breath into you, and you will come alive. After this happens, you will know that I am the Eternal."
Ezekiel 37:4-5 The Voice

Thirty Three

Find Me, Finding You

I see you, Daughter.

When you look at yourself in the mirror, you are sometimes flooded with memories of shame, disappointment, and un-forgiveness. I am whispering to you, "I love you. I am proud of you. You are forgiven."

I hear you, Daughter. I hear the words and lies that have been spoken over you; how they sometimes replay in your mind creating white noise of confusion and chaos. I am bringing angels to your side to play trumpets of joy that fill you with peace, understanding, and direction!

I feel you, Daughter. I feel the pain of past decisions and choices you struggle to believe could ever be undone. I am coming beside you, holding you, walking with you, carrying you while we work through the pain t ogether. Daughter, you are My Beloved.

———

There once was a shepherd with a hundred lambs, but one of his lambs wandered away and was lost. So the shepherd left the ninety-nine lambs out in the open field and searched in the wilderness for that one lost lamb. He didn't stop until he finally found it. With exuberant joy he raised it up and placed it on his shoulders, carrying it back with cheerful delight!
Luke 15:4-5 TPT

Thirty Four

Dahlia Delight

Have you ever looked at a bouquet of dahlias?

I created them in all shapes, sizes and colors. They are each so unique that you may think they are different kinds of flowers, but they're not!

I have sometimes heard you compare yourself with others, wishing you were taller or shorter, had curly hair or straight hair, were skinnier or more muscular. But, My dear, when I knit you together, I did not make a mistake.

I designed you so uniquely to display My glory! Can you imagine if one of the dahlias hid itself because it didn't look like the others, or shriveled back because it didn't want to stand out? No way! The same it should be with you, My girl. Now, go out and be boldly, beautifully YOU.

I thank you, God, for making me so mysteriously complex! Everything you do is marvelously breathtaking. It simply amazes me to think about it! How thoroughly you know me Lord! Psalm 139:14,15 TPT

Thirty Five

My Love, Like Water

My love is the water: the trickle; the roar.

My love is the wave overtaking the shore. My love engulfs you without a trace - I find no fault with you washed in My grace.

A spring of water creates a serene sound. A waterfall spans the heights, aggressively plunging over boulders and crashing to the sea. Niagara Falls demolishes anything in its way. As the water, I can both whisper and roar in My passionate pursuit of your heart.

I can usher in peace, and I can violently tear down barriers between us. I can wreck you with truth, then tenderly kiss your tears away.

My deep need calls out to the deep kindness of your love. Your waterfall of weeping sent waves of sorrow over my soul, carrying me away, cascading over me like a thundering cataract. Yet all day long God's promises of love pour over me. Through the night I sing his songs, for my prayer to God has become my life.
Psalm 42:7-8 TPT

Thirty Six

Best Friends

YIt's tempting to turn to a good friend first when you need help.

I placed trusted friends in your life for that reason. But, when it comes to the supernatural touch that your heart, mind, and body desperately needs, I want to be your first responder.

Are you facing stress, illness, loss, or pressure? I am the only one who can lavish you at a depth that transforms. I am able to change things. The relief you are looking for is found in Me.

It's My supernatural touch you need today. I want to hold you. I want to wrap Myself around you. I am your proud defender! I am your healer! I am your joy! I am your dream designer! I am your best friend. Lean on me. What do you need today, baby?

I have never called you 'servants,' because a master doesn't confide in his servants, and servants don't always understand what the master is doing. But I call you my most intimate friends, for I reveal to you everything that I've heard from my Father.
John 15:15 TPT

Thirty Seven

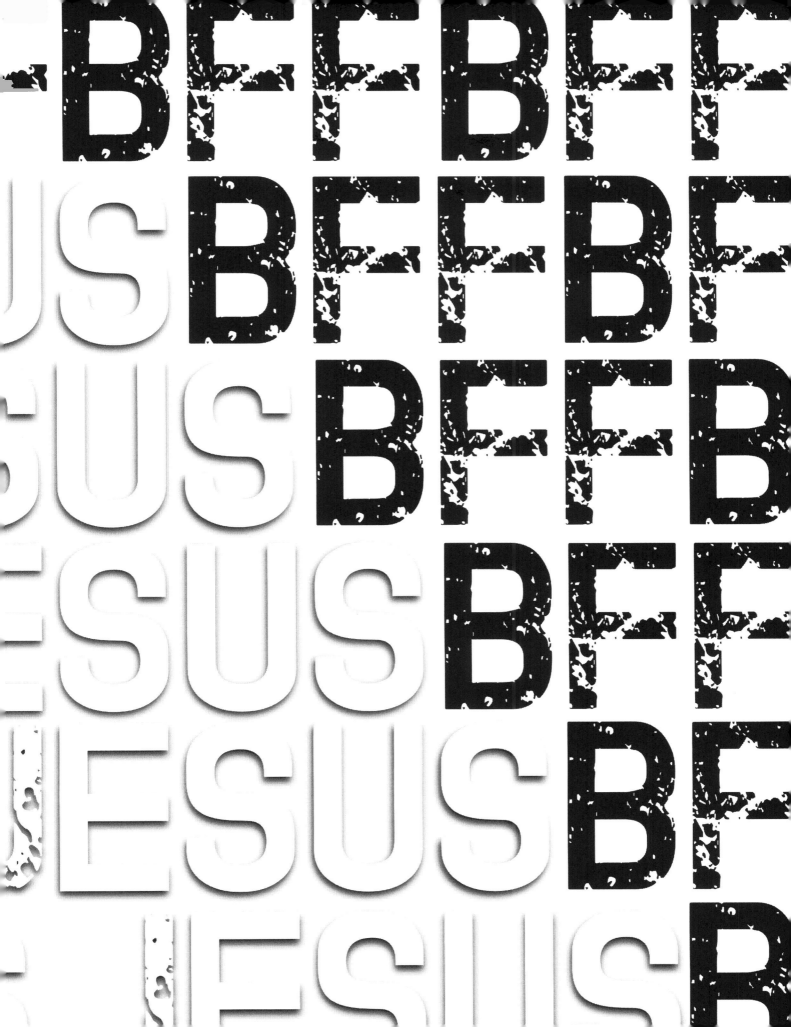

Glory To Glory

I am extending My grace and favor to you.

Step into it - it's yours. I paid for it! In fact, the influence of your house is expanding because of the grace I have extended to you!

Reach out to Me without fear or shame. I am near to you - as close as your breath. Let Me help you; let Me love you; receive My favor and miracles.

My grace is sufficient for your every need, desire, and dream.
Follow Me. Listen to My voice. I'm leading you from glory to glory!

We can all draw close to him with the veil removed from our faces. And with no veil we all become like mirrors who brightly reflect the glory of the Lord Jesus. We are being transfigured into his very image as we move from one brighter level of glory to another. And this glorious transfiguration comes from the Lord, who is the Spirit.
2 Corinthians 3:18 TPT

Thirty Eight

Proud Father

Daughter, I have watched you grow. I've walked with you and been with you every step and you've made Me so proud.

You've believed in Me, Daughter; and I have always believed in you. I marvel at the way you think. I'm amazed by your fearlessness. I cherish the way you honor Me with your childlike faith and thank Me for all I have given you.

I want you to know that all that I have, I have given to you. All that you could ever need is yours. Right now, you may not be able to fathom all that this means; that's okay! I will open your eyes and ears more fully to understand the riches of your inheritance. Trust Me, you have it all!

You're My prized possession; My diamond; My pearl; My precious gem. I love to watch you walk into a room knowing exactly who you are; whose you are. I marvel at your radiant light. Everywhere you go, you shine bright. I'm so proud.

I pray that the Father of glory, the God of our Lord Jesus Christ, would impart to you the riches of the Spirit of wisdom and the Spirit of revelation to know him through your deepening intimacy with him. I pray that the light of God will illuminate the eyes of your imagination, flooding you with light, until you experience the full revelation of the hope of his calling —that is, the wealth of God's glorious inheritances that he finds in us, his holy ones!
Ephesians 1:17-18 TPT

Thirty Nine

Becoming Bright

I am so proud of the woman you're becoming!

I I've watched over your every breath and am so pleased to watch you flourish into the woman you're becoming. You shine SO brightly. You reflect the light of My love, and because of this, you make others want to get to know Me. You make Me so happy!

My deepest desire is for us to get to know each other more deeply. Nothing you've done, or will do, can separate you from the love I have for you.

Look with wonder at the depth of the Father's marvelous love that he has lavished on us! He has called us and made us his very own beloved children. The reason the world doesn't recognize who we are is that they didn't recognize him. Beloved, we are God's children right now; however, it is not yet apparent what we will become. But we do know that when it is finally made visible, we will be just like him, for we will see him as he truly is.
1 John 3:1-2

Forty

I See You, Child

I see you, child. I see each and every detail of you through the filter of love: your face, your features, your emotions, your desires.

I see you, as a mother gazes into the face of her newborn baby. My love for you is as thick as the fog in the mountains! It permeates the atmosphere and rests like dew on your skin. Can you feel it?

My love for you is so lavish that My fountain of forgiveness overflows into each day and each moment. It never runs dry and always overflows its basin. You are beautiful, My child.

Sit with Me and breathe in My love. Rest. Relax your mind, the ambitions and to-dos you hold so closely, and rest in My lavish, unconditional love. You are My treasure, My lovely one.

God, give me mercy from your fountain of forgiveness! I know your abundant love is enough to wash away my guilt. Because your compassion is so great, take away this shameful guilt of sin. Forgive the full extent of my rebellious ways, and erase this deep stain on my conscience.
Psalm 51:1-2 TPT

Forty One

Radiant Hope

I am Hope!

If I am in you, and I am Hope, then hope is never lost. If you feel fearful to hope again, share your fears with Me. I am here waiting, full of hope for you.

Like a newborn baby in the arms of her Mother, look to the light on My face and see the hope that radiates from Me to you. You are the promise of new birth fulfilled! Like the first signs of spring, the budding trees and the daffodils blooming from their winter sleep, so I am calling forth the hope in your heart to awaken from its slumber.

I want to lavish you with hope so that it radiates from you as My face is turned toward you in favor and love.

Now may God, the inspiration and fountain of hope, fill you to overflowing with uncontainable joy and perfect peace as you trust in him. And may the power of the Holy Spirit continually surround your life with his super-abundance until you radiate with hope!
Romans 15:13 TPT

Forty Two

Ask Me

You have questions; I have answers — all the answers you could ever need!

It's My joy to give you My wisdom, counsel and instruction, so please don't shrink back! I am honored when you open your heart to Me.

Ask Me about anything and everything! No question or request is too big or too small; too trivial or complex. I will listen intently and respond to you in My perfect timing and way. You can expect My timely replies!

The very act of you asking makes Me smile and invites Me to lavish you with blessings I have in store especially for you. I am the God who approaches and is not silent (Psalm 50:3)!

I am sent to announce a new season of Yahweh's grace and a time of God's recompense on his enemies, to comfort all who are in sorrow, to strengthen those crushed by despair who mourn in Zion-to give them a beautiful bouquet in the place of ashes, the oil of bliss instead of tears, and the mantle of joyous praise instead of the spirit of heaviness. Because of this, they will be known as Mighty Oaks of Righteousness planted by Yahweh as a living display of his glory.
Isaiah 61:2-3

Forty Three

"Remain" To Be Changed

I don't want to fix you; I want to love everything about you into the right places and spaces.

It's My love that changes things. As you allow Me to love you, the things you don't like about yourself are changed. Let Me love those things into something beautiful today. Yes, you can trust Me in this! As you remain in Me, you will be changed. It's not something you strive to obtain; it's something you receive in My presence.

I love you too much to leave you the same - I have plans to take you from glory to glory in this season!

The words I have spoken over you have already cleansed you. So you must remain in life-union with me, for I remain in life-union with you. For as a branch severed from the vine will not bear fruit, so your life will be fruitless un less you live your life intimately joined to mine.
John 15:3-4 TPT

Forty Four

Details, Details

Trust Me in the details of your life.

There is nothing too small, too insignificant or too trivial. That which concerns you, concerns Me. I am great enough to speak the earth into existence, and yet I can count the stars of the most distant galaxy.

When a bird falls to the ground, I recognize it. How much more do I concern myself over you? You are My beloved child. I am YOUR Father. I see your mind wandering, attempting to figure out your next steps. My promises remain.

I will never leave you or forsake you. As you seek Me and acknowledge Me in your daily decisions, I will direct your path. I am in the details of your life, working in all things for your good. You can trust Me!

*Trust in the Lord completely, and do not rely on your own opinions.
With all your heart rely on him to guide you, and he will lead you in every decision you make. Become intimate with him in whatever you do, and he will lead you wherever you go. Proverbs 3:5-6 TPT*

Forty Five

Allow Me To Interrupt

Slow down, My love. Just breathe.

I notice when you start to feel burnt out, you begin to believe you have nothing left to give. I notice when you begin to compare yourself, you begin to believe everyone has it together but you. You try to stay strong and feel shame when you're unable to pull up any longer. It's a vicious cycle that I'm happy to interrupt!

When the lies from the enemy creep in, remember: I say the opposite. When you hear, "You're a bad friend," I am whispering to your spirit, "You're an incredible friend!" When Satan whispers, "You can't, you're too burnt out," I'm whispering, "YOU CAN! I'll supply you with everything you need!"

But he answered me, "My grace is always more than enough for you, and my power finds its full expression through your weakness." So I will celebrate my weaknesses, for when I'm weak I sense more deeply the mighty power of Christ living in me.
2 Corinthians 12:9 TPT

Forty Six

Healing Hope

I see and feel your pain, and I want to heal all your brokenness.

Tune your ears to My voice and rest in My peace. Spend your free moments listening for Me. Breathe Me in and out. I will show you how to get your physical body to line up. I am The Healer; The Great Physician.

Daughter, it may seem like this world is closing in, but I see you. I have ordered your steps, and when you misstep, I have already ordered your way back to Me. My only limitation is the gift of free will I gave you.

Seek Me fully and you will find Me: I am Hope; Peace; Grace; Joy, and Love. I created you to walk in all of these things and more. Every step towards Me brings you further into the fullness of who you are created to be. Keep you eyes locked on Mine. I will hold your gaze.
I see you as I created you to be: one who lives and speaks life. Your healing does not stop with you; it will carry healing to others around you. You are designed to breathe life into those around you.

Trust in the Lord completely, and do not rely on your own opinions. With all your heart rely on him to guide you, and he will lead you in every decision you make. Become intimate with him in whatever you do, and he will lead you wherever you go….
Proverbs 3:5-6 TPT

Forty Seven

Gentle Gardener

I am the Gentle Gardener, tending to the soil of your heart.

I am not intimidated by any amount of wilting or overgrowth. I can work wonders with the crushed, tattered and most damaged places.

I want to walk through your heart's garden and refresh you today. Let Me pour My love over you delicately, as from a red watering can in My hand. I want to freshen up the weary places and bring the withering back to life. I see the areas inside your heart that need to be watered.

Come walk with Me. Talk with Me about these places. You may think they are lifeless beyond repair, but I want you to know – resurrecting the dead is what I do best.

Looking at his gentle face I see such fullness of emotion. Like a lovely garden where f ragrant spices grow— what a man! No one speaks words so anointed as this one— words that both pierce and heal, words like lilies dripping with myrrh.
Song of Songs 5:13 TPT

Forty Eight

Breathtaking Bride

I am calling you deeper into the heat of My love for you.

My love will melt your heart like wax, Beloved. You can rest upon Me, allowing your heart to become One with Mine. My eyes like fire are locked on YOU: perfectly designed, assigned and prepared for Me, your Bridegroom. Your desire to be wholly Mine has captured My heart, and I am seized breathless in elation and anticipation for you. I am coming for you!

Surrender yourself to the image of who you are in My eyes. Shatter every restraining definition of My Love and advance into the majesty and purity of My redeeming, secure and empowering love for you. Receive My passion as a Bride receives her Bridegroom.

"For you reach into my heart with one flash of your eyes. I am undone by your love, my beloved, my equal, my bride. You leave me breathless from your worshiping eyes, for you have stolen my heart. I am held hostage by your love and by the graces of righteousness shining upon you."
Song of Songs 4:9 TPT

Forty Nine

Unspeakable Joy

Imagine a life of unspeakable joy ~ a joy that exists deep within you; that rises up in your soul and never leaves you.

Hear Me, beautiful one of Mine: a journey of joy awaits you. Right now in My Presence, you can feast continually on My joy! There is no life circumstance that can offer the joy I desire to lavish you with. No riches or success; treasures; people; health, or any other thing in the world can assure the unspeakable joy I am promising you.

Joy is a fruit of knowing Me intimately. The more time you spend with Me, the more you will come to know and treasure My love; My ways; My promises; My voice, and My truths. As you allow My joy to be your strength, it will begin to explode in your spirit, bursting forth no matter what is going on around you!

As you spend time in My Presence, My fullness of joy will be yours and heaviness will melt away. Yes, through our time together, you will become an overflowing wellspring of joy!

"Let joy be your continual feast." 1 Thessalonians 5:16 TPT

Fifty

Remember Me, Your Rescue

I want to lift up your head and renew your faith in Me today, My beauty.

Let's take a walk down memory lane, and allow Me to remind you of who I have been for you:

Remember that time you felt so weak that you wondered if you could make it, and I showed Myself strong within you?
Remember that season you desperately cried out for My help, and I answered your prayer so specifically?

Remember when you wanted to sit in the dark with a blanket over your head, and I became your hiding place?
I was there for you then, and I will be again. I'm coming to your rescue.

When I screamed out, "Lord I'm doomed" your fiery love was stirred and you raced to my rescue. When my thoughts were out of control, the soothing comfort of your presence calmed me down and overwhelmed me with delight.
Psalm 94:18-19 TPT

Fifty One

Let's Settle This

Your sins are forgiven, so no more bringing them up to Me, okay?

I do not condemn you! My Son dealt with sin once and for all on the cross. I don't count your sins against you, so there's no reason to hold them against yourself any longer! When you hold onto condemnation, you let go of My grace - both cannot fit in your heart at the same time.

Let Me help you let go of self-condemnation and cling to the freedom of My grace. I have made all things new!

Now that that's settled, can we spend some time together? I'm so proud of who you are!

And God has made all things new, and reconciled us to himself, and given us the ministry of reconciling others to God. In other words, it was through the Anointed One that God was shepherding the world, not even keeping records of their transgressions, and he has entrusted to us the ministry of opening the door of reconciliation to God.
2 Corinthians 5:18-19 TPT

Fifty Two

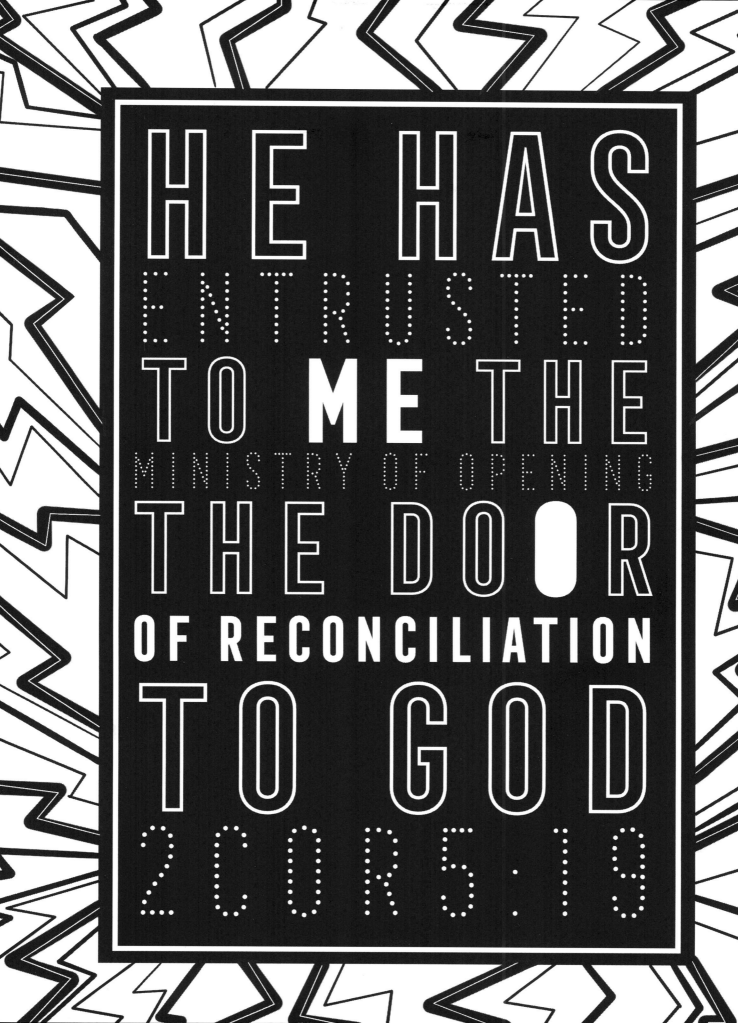

Connect with Us

FACEBOOK / INSTAGRAM / EMAIL
@tetelestaiministries
@hervoice_movement
admin@tetelestaiministries.com

TETELESTAI

JENNY DONNELLY AND
TETELESTAI MINISTRIES INC.